Finding My Wheels Through Poetry

Emily Bonner

BookLeaf
Publishing

India | USA | UK

Finding My Wheels Through Poetry © 2022
Emily Bonner

Presentation by *BookLeaf Publishing*

Web: www.bookleafpub.com

E-mail: info@bookleafpub.com

ISBN: 9789357448628

First edition 2022

DEDICATION

To my mum Frances, who believed in me from the very start - her spirit keeps me strong

ACKNOWLEDGEMENT

Thank you to all those beautiful souls that have inspired me, taught me and touched the very core of my being in some way, shape or form. Some of these poems may not exist if it had not of been for your input.

PREFACE

So, it has become apparent over the years that I have a way with words...

I started out with writing poems as a kid. My sister had purchased a small autograph book for me, and I was mesmerised by the blank sheets of paper all different colours of the rainbow like. The first set of pages were coloured orange. I never met anyone famous so fake signatures would appear in the book at random places. I'd also scrawl in it, I liked to write my name, a lot! In fact, I still do that to this day.
Now what's the meaning behind this? Is there some subconscious part of my being that is still trying to fathom out the name given to me as a new-born? More than likely.
So, it was this very book that I ripped out an orange sheet from and wrote my first poem.
I don't remember writing that first poem "What A Day" but my mum found it and kept it as it had made her laugh.
It was tucked safely away in her wigging box for eons. She'd find it after a period of time had passed along with other scraps of my work and proclaimed that she was collecting them for a future book.

Thinking about it, that first poem was probably
written on a bleak winter weekend, stuck in the
"coal hole" and well you guessed it this is the
book my mum predicted I'd write.

I first found my passion for word aged 9 in Mrs
Davies's class on a Friday afternoon before our
weekly 'Celebration Assembly'.
I loved 'Celebration Assembly' because it
occupied the final hour of school for the week
and Friday nights were swim nights and I'd get
to go to 'Woollies' for a bag of pick 'n' mix to
munch on after on the long walk back home.
I remember the creative writing class well.
We had to write a piece on a given subject, it
was my first introduction to this type of writing.
Suddenly it all came to me, from where at that
time I couldn't tell you, but I got very excited
'cos I was thinking to myself this is bloody good
ja! I am writing amazingly well! It's all fitting so
perfectly together!
It was such a moment in my life writing a line
something akin to "snowflakes grow up the
glistening wall" that I still remember it to this
day.
The seed was sown, and I was so proud of me
work that I couldn't wait to thrust it into 'The
Welsh Dragon's' lap before hot footing it down

the link corridor to the hall to celebrate the week just gone.

I can't remember what she made of it now. She was the teacher that told me mum I was like part of the furniture as I was so quiet but it was one of my favourite years in school as it was the first year in middle school and we had loads of different classes to attend like pottery and art but more so the fact I could go home for my lunch, it made such a difference to my emotional state being away from the other kids and the noise of the dining room. I also never went hungry! I digress.

"I need more material, get writing '2 sticks Bonner'".

Over the years mum would request I write more poems for her so she could continue to collect them for this book that she'll now sadly never get to see.

'Em's Book of Poems' she'd call it in which I've now renamed 'Finding My Wheels Through Poetry' because at the time of writing this here preface, I am awaiting my first wheelchair and my life of poetry thus far is about finding my feet.

So here goes the thing...

I look back at my poetry from my early days and
I can instantly tell where my headspace was at
that moment in time.
I can't help but feel that they were pretty bleak, I
even cringe a little bit when reading them back,
but they were just reflecting that time period of
my past and to stay authentic to myself it would
be unjust for me not to include them. Plus, I try
not to take heed of my ego mind these days.
They were young Emily's poems. The Emily
who hated the world and herself and Christmas!
Ok, I still don't go crazy over Christmas but
that's because of commercialisation and the
hype and the fact that fecking people start
talking about it in bleedin' September and it's all
about you should buy this and that and do this or
that and spend time with family and make
memories blah blah blah.
Honestly, I don't like the pretence around it
either. Let's play "happy families" and all that
lark. I much rather spend my time in a soup
kitchen talking to real people who I've never
met before and listening to their stories with an
open heart. So there goes my opinionated self!

Basically, I'm not here to "cherry pick" the good
stuff, you my dear reader are getting the whole

bloody lot, warts 'n' all, the good, the bad and the ugly!

I'm determined not to live my life in fear of people's opinions. Better to shit oneself than to worry about shitting oneself as goes the quote I happened upon a few weeks back.

In this book me heart will be on my proverbial sleeve so come wipe ya nose on it and let's dance!

Back then when I started out on me poetry journey I wasn't in an environment where I could exactly thrive.

I was somewhat restricted by the childhood home, past conditioning and had a victim mentality. My childhood wasn't exactly bad, but neither would I class it as very good either. It had its moments shall we say, and I was depressed at times, suffering with mental health and behavioural issues. I also liked to keep myself to myself.

As the old saying goes if a flower doesn't thrive then change its environment. We live and learn and continuously so.

I got back into my poetry a bit around the time of my muscular dystrophy diagnosis, and these were slightly more light-hearted and humorous with the odd exception.

My big coping mechanism is the old humour!
Laughing in the face of adversity and using
writing as not only a form of self-expression but
also for healing. I am always laughing at myself.
I find myself rather funny at times. I have even
wet myself laughing at myself which in turn
made me laugh even harder. Laughter certainly
is the best medicine except for incontinence.
Am I unstable? Nah, I'm saner than most.

I was to have a difficult decade with a lot
happening in quick succession.
There was the muscular dystrophy, I got sacked
for using the word "tosser", spent a year
unemployed (so I went fishing), me nan became
unrecognisable in her dementia then died, I had
to find my own pad which was a blessing if not
tough at first as my wages barely covered my
rent. I went hungry again periodically. No harm
done.
Then mum died, maybe I'll write about this one
day, if I ever feel ready.
I later moved home and then a long-term
relationship broke down.
These events I am now grateful for as each one
has taught me many valuable lessons in life.
Listening to a podcast recently on breathwork
and rebirthing the chap mentions that he was
blessed with pain and suffering, and I can totally

relate as this is how I feel about past experiences. I digress again. Maybe I should just let the poetry speak for itself?

It was after mum passed away that I rediscovered my poems that she'd saved. They were no longer in her wigging box but tucked away in the back of a notebook waiting patiently for me and for this very book. She also gifted me a few pages of her own writings which is amazing as she was not what she'd term a writer. These few pages offer such a profound insight to how my mum was in the process of discovering what I have come to discover in recent years. She reflects back on her past conditioning with such diffidence. The analogy I like to think of is that she had the key to the door but didn't know how to use it.

It warms my very heart to know that she would be so pleased that I am finally writing this book. I'm also writing this for her and because of her. You are only reading this because of Frances.

I've also been penning a few poems over the last couple of years, and some I've especially created to complete this book.

I've certainly experienced a shift in my
spirituality, there is now a deep-rooted inner
peace within me and ample love in my heart.
Look at how the lotus blooms in muddy waters.
This is how I see myself on my journey through
these life experiences, and maybe you'll see this
reflected through my word as the poetry evolves.
So, join me if you will as I find my wheels
through poetry and maybe one day you never
know I may well find my feet again!

What A Day (as written as a child)

What a day it is today
Yes what a day it is today
Oh what a day it is today
It's a bloody awful day today!

It's Christmas (as written as a child)

Same old wrap
Same old crap
Same old cards
Bloody charades
Too much to eat
Same old meat
Some old stocking
Who needs a socking?
TV shite
Turkish Delight
Grey old weather
Birds of a feather
Twelve mince pies
Bloodshot eyes
Depression and SAD
Drives you mad
Same old cheer
Every sodding year
Merry Christmas!

Pied (as written as a child)

How's your son restless one?
Is he back on the crack?
Or had another schizo attack?
Does he take gay pride in his stride?
The pale, blue-eyed, frightened child

How's your daughter restless one?
Settled down and out on the town?
Or feeling down?
Is it denied what's going on inside?
The dark, brown-eyed frightened child

Strimmin' in Suburbia

Strimmin' in suburbia
Every weekend morn
Don't care about disturbing ya
Got to tend to ma lawn
Weeds are not allowed here
Got to keep it trim
Just perfect grass no fear
All they wanna do is strim, strim, strim

Then out comes the mower
The daisies do despair
As them blades do lower
The geezer doesn't seem to care
Weeds are not allowed here
And flowers are classed as weeds
Just perfect grass no fear
So, nothing gets to seed

Ode to The Job Centre

No fucking work for you or I
It will certainly be like this until you die
Another day wasted; another day gone
"Have your circumstances changed" they ask
"No" you reply "kiss my arse"
The box is ticked, your payment goes through,
you leave demoralised and angry too
You go home, you sit, you stare, you start to
wonder and begin not to care
Three days later you get your dosh
Just enough to buy some nosh
Signing on every other week
No fucking luck with the jobs you seek
No fucking work for you or I
It will probably be like this until you die

Gammy Legs

Gammy legs like soft boiled eggs
And bits sticking out like a freak show
This is how my body is and
Always on the go slow

Muscles wasting what am I facing
A life of death and decay?
No, no I cry I must go on I won't let this get in
the way

Falling over like the cliffs of Dover
Is a daily occurrence for me
And also having a weak old bladder that
struggles to hold in the wee!

But I am strong inside and I will not hide
Myself away to rot
I'm going out there in the big wide world and
going to face the lot!

Farty Bum

Farty bum bum in my bed
Then he grabs my bloody
head

And holds it down under the cover
God I really do have to suffer

But it's so amusing I can't help but giggle
Even though I'm trying to wiggle

Away from the stench away from the stink
My eyes are watering I can't not blink

It's so pungent there is no air
He's still a grabbing me by the hair

Finally, I manage to fight
Out into the open into the light

I'm free for a while until next time at least
But I guarantee the next ones a beast!

The Stairs Are No More

Today the stairs defeated me
And in my mind, it was repeated to me

"The time is coming more quickly than
expected, than anticipated..."

It's related, even correlated

And I'm certainly not conceited
Of my failings underpinned by the degradation
of my muscles

Life's tussles
We must face
For if not conquered by the correct mentality
We will lose the ability and the willpower to
carry on

Sun Rising

Louie, Luca and then my mo'
One, two, three, all in a row

And Mr Orr is by her side
Looking across the vista wide

An empty space is to her right
Leaving a clear and spacious sight

But no one yet lies passed her feet
I wonder who she will one day meet

Seven hundred and fifty odd bods lie
Each one wondering why they had to die

Some in woodland and some in the meadow
On the ridge and in the furrow

As the heavy clay soil is again unearthed
Bit by bit and slightly disturbed

Another hole appears 6ft deep
It is later filled, and people weep

A mass of earth soon piles high
Underneath a moonlit sky

In time it will settle and then will be found
A tree or wildflowers along the ground

As these dead do nourish
All shall flourish on this special piece of sacred
land

Ode to Oxford's Indoor Market

Oh, the whiff of fish did hit you as you entered
off the street
People hustling and bustling, the sound of
hurried feet

I'm sure there was a cobbler mending leather
shoes
And also, a cheese counter selling cheddars,
washed rinds and blues

Then the Bonner's veg stall with all its variety
One of the many businesses serving society

I remember the floor of the butchers covered in
sawdust
And a bloke chopping up a carcass - lamb chops
a must!

There were live lobsters stacked at the
fishmonger along with crabs and eels
An eclectic mix of sea life ready for making
many meals

But we only went to Nash's for a traditional
lardy cake
It was me Nan's favourite as she couldn't be
bothered to bake

We took one home for her neighbour Mrs Tuzzio
The other we kept for ourselves and demolished
it pronto!

2020 Vision

Each and every one of us holding a virtual hand
This ain't no disaster
It's a cleansing of the land

Some may clap the NHS
And others bang their lids
People standing in the street's men, women, dogs
and kids

As air pollution decreases
The Himalayas emerge
Showing their strength and beauty, secrets on the
verge

Clear waters now run in Venice first time in an
age
No more millions of tourists
A turning of the page

Nature is now healing
From devastation caused by man
In a way it's payback time
It's all part of the plan

Sadly, lives will be lost

From one thing or another
Hand gel can't save us all
And nor can they Holy Mother

So, what will get us through?
The power of the mind
Living in the moment
And always being kind

A collective of positivity connecting to the
source
Being non-judgemental
Will keep you all on course

So 'Breathe Motherfucker!'
Just like Wim Hof says
And find a productive way
To while away the days

Let us be creative
And discover who we are
Everybody matters
Those close and those afar

All rise together guys
And be a shining light
This time is a blessing
My love to you day and night

The Rousham Tree

Oh, how this tree talks to me
Instantly drawn in I am
By its haunting beauty dominating the
landscape
And by a familiarity that connects me to my
mum
Who sadly left this plane far too prematurely
It was in all her favourite tree

Oh, how this tree talks to me

It's a stark reminder that death is life and life is
death
One cannot be without the other

My muscles may have withered like the here
limbs of this tree
But that light is still shining brightly just as the
sun peaks out from a cloud
It too shines for everyone and on everyone
There is always light and there is always hope

Oh, how this tree talks to me

Here the tree stands tall and proud

It is not ashamed of its current state
It is not concerned with the opinions or
judgments of others
It just is a tree that is still firmly grounded after
chaos that ultimately brought its demise
Although I bet if you look closely there is life in
that tree somewhere

More life than a sleeping soul

Probably…

Oh, how this tree talks to me

"Sunny" Nunny

So, I grew up in Nunny along the thoroughfare
'Tween the rough estate up top and the town
centre down there

By the borough football club
So, Saturdays were a treat
The coppers would be on horseback
And they'd also close the street

Fights would often breakout
Especially if they'd lost
Hooligans ran down the road
With snooker balls in socks

These got smashed through pub windows
And riots would begin
However, if the mood was good
They'd celebrate a win

By pulling down their trousers
And flashing to the cars
Looking out the window
You'd get an eye full of drunken arse

This all happened on

The mini roundabout
The traffic would start a hooting
And often people would shout

Obscenities were regular
And domestics frequent too
Once me neighbour's girlfriend
Went crazy and caused such a do

We even had kitchen knives
Tossed over the garden wall
Or left on top of a pillar
That warranted a call

To the local bobbies
Who often on the beat
Would be searching the front gardens
And all around the street

The chopper was a regular
That helped them in their plight
To find the runaway fugitives
By using the search light

Once we got a burgled
And they stole all me dad's tools
Using me sister's Mini
To get away with the "Crown Jewels"

Then there is the hole
In a pane of glass
Made with an air rifle
Some people have the brass

Bodies floating in the cut
And handbags dumped there too
Murders were occasional
And crimes more than a few

Walking home from school
A guy came up to me
Put his arm around my shoulder
Which made me shout and flee

A drunkard turned up at the door
It was only 8am
Howling for us to let him in
He thought it wasn't us but them

He started staggering in the road
So again, the cops were called
Next thing he's arrested
They were obviously enthralled

So, I grew up in Nunny along the thoroughfare
'Tween the rough estate up top
And the town centre down there

It certainly was a colourful time
And a lot of sights were seen
Now I've escaped to a better place where the
grass is always green

Ode to MDSC

When we all got thrown together
About a year ago
This social group got created
And some troublemakers I got to know

In truth they aren't all that bad
But some are worse than others
More like a family to me
My MDSC sisters' 'n' brothers'

There's Rob the sunbather
Who snook off to Lanzarote
He made it over just in time
Before the world went potty

Neil got a lambing
But the chicks were off their lay
He started to learn the keyboard
And we've yet to hear him play!

Judy, she's the daredevil
Jumped out of a plane
She landed firmly on the ground
So, we'll get to see her again

Now Bryan is the Villa fan
And we'll say no more on that
He went to the nudist beach
And used his Villa hat!

Andy sits there pulling faces
When his camera doesn't work
Hobgoblin firmly in his hand
And we've even seen him twerk!

Diana scrapes the data
And forges cheques we think
Cleverly designing gadgets
To print before you can blink

Ian is the chatty one
But he's been outdone by Paul
The cows came home long ago
And technology he has it all

Not forgetting David
Who's into golf n bridge
Likes to go to Sainsbury's
To stock up the old fridge

Annette moved to Cheltenham
Maybe for the races?
But hopefully we will see her again
And all these familiar faces

But what I really want to say
Is that I'm blessed to of met you all
When we all got thrown together
In this much needed wakeup call

And for those I haven't mentioned
Know that I love ya too
Let's keep laughing together
For humour is long overdue

The Lesson Of The Apple Tree

I once had an apple tree
And then my drive got done

I wanted to save its life
But suddenly it was gone

The digger took over before I could ask
To move my apple tree across the piece of grass

A lesson of detachment from The Universe
I had to let it go and so I chose not to curse

Several months later and this is what I find
A host of baby saplings completely blows my
mind

So by learning to let go and learning to detach
I was shown that Mother Nature is certainly no
match

My front garden wants to be an orchard, it seems

To which I shall oblige, with a picture of my
dreams

Inspiration

Oh, how life and death is only separated by one
short breath
Yet that is what connects us all
Not just to each other but
Mind, body and spirit are sewn together
Through the simplicity that is breathing

Although it can also have its complexities
Peeling away the layers the deeper we get
We see this in its truest form, but then a deep
rooted sense of security appears
Oh, the beauty of the breath!

Yet it can also cause us distress
The panic when suddenly it's not there anymore
The old friend that seemingly left when one
literally cannot live without their power
A force to be reckoned with

And also, a gentle caress when relaxation feels
it's way into the very core of being
There's that purity, coherence with the heart
A fluid undertone of synchronicity
Then there is bliss as we return home

See these dualistic tendencies of the breath
And the power created outwardly and internally?

Breath

It's the beginning
And it's the end
And yet it's also everything else in-between

Grief

The cloud of grieving doth shadow the mind
Only a memory that you left behind

But not just that, an imprint too
You are a part of me as I am a part of you

Physically not here yet you are everywhere it
seems
United and coming together I meet you in my
dreams

And as we walk together on this trodden Earth
Figuratively hand-in-hand across the Universe

I know you are always with me if only I do look
At all the sights around me and in every single
nook

Though more powerful is the feeling always in
my heart
And that my dear one can never keep us apart

For this reason only, I cannot always be sad
I treasure these moments forever and yet pine
for what we once had

Although I know that is just attachment and our
bond can never break
Karmically tied together waiting to re-awake

I love it best when I hear your words come
through the voice of me
And even the voice of you coming through the
words of me

And in those precious moments I too can also
perceive
All the lessons you came to teach me and what I
was meant to receive

With your old soul attributes and a sense of
wisdom singing
This isn't but the end it's merely the very
beginning

We hold a piece of each other that's true
As you took a part of me and left behind a part
of you

Ego and Flow

When ego subsides and when ego relents
There's no hesitation or concern for events

No um-ing or ah-ing, no if's and no but's
All the ego does is keep us in ruts

We don't weigh up the options or ask questions
inside
That analytical stuff is for when ego abides

And when ego is rife, we struggle to see
What's important in life and just how to be

The path ahead can be cloudy or clear
But often we find ourselves living in fear

So, stay true to your heart and then you shall feel
This flow of pure magic that seems so unreal

The flow will grow stronger, and ego will drop
Into a place where you know, it may even stop

For a short while at least so you can fathom out
Essentially all that is and what life's all about

Let intuitive feelings take over knowing there's
nothing to resist
Just go into the space of unadulterated bliss

Everything will then just fall into place
If you just trust and let life go at its own gentle
pace

Flow is easy and you know what to do
You just do it, no what if, what now or how so

You just know

So go with the flow!

Moon Hunting

There you are! Beauty of the deep night
Big and bold, dominating the sky and reflecting
back the sunlight
I see you; I can't miss you, just follow that
silvery glow and then you do show
Your beauty of this deep night

Where are you? Beauty of the deep night
Now you are shy and hidden by thick cloud
Or even hiding between the trees and on
emerging from their shroud
I see you; I can't miss you, just follow that
silvery glow and then you do show
Your beauty of this deep night

There you are! Beauty of the deep night
A thick, golden crescent of mighty gold
Hugging the horizon, you are down low and
won't withhold your inner peace truth be told
I see you; I can't miss you, just follow that
golden glow and then you do show
Your beauty of this deep night

Where are you? Beauty of the deep night

The sky is dark, the stars be bright, you are new
and out of sight, wishes made do come true oh
our foresight
I feel you; I can't miss you, just follow that
darkness and even yet you don't show you are
still there emanating
Your glow and beauty of this deep night

On Me Knees

Whistling wind comes through the trees
And nearly brings me to my knees
If only I could rise back up
Then down I'd go in this autumn breeze

To scoop up leaves and toss them up high
Above my head and into the sky
If only I could rise them up
Above my chest, my arms I'd fly

Then down I'd roll and tucked into a ball
I'd bounce around in the fall
If only I could rise to walk
My legs I'd move and up from a crawl

I'd stand again to hop, skip 'n' jump
Over the twigs and occasional stump
If only I could move about
Then I'd play all day and out of the slump

Of my body I'd rise then my back be straight
I'd stand up tall and walk, no gait
If only I was not diseased
I could do all this but as my fate

Is to rely on sticks and braces and wheels
To get about safely and up off my heels
"If only" isn't a statement I now make
As I am content with life and how I feels

About the beauty of all that is
Around me, over me, under me, nature's kiss
Now only I can be just me
Then up I shall rise in all of this

Wheels

Grounded in the root, we are
Stuck in our ways and out from afar

Flooding the sacral, we feel
A huge wave of emotion that we need to heal

Burning the solar plexus, we do
Self-assurance in creating the new

Soaring above the heart, we love
Compassion and empathy that fits like a glove

Finding that space in the throat we speak
Through our voice we surely seek

By lighting the third eye, we see
An intuitive glance at what might be

And finally

Thinking of the crown, we just know
As above and so below…